The Ferris Wheel

Jesse Rey Whipple

Janus Visions Press

The Ferris Wheel. Copyright © 2017 by Jesse Rey Whipple. All rights reserved. No part of this book may be used or reproduced in any manner without written permission except in the case of brief quotations embodied in critical articles and reviews.

ISBN: 978-0-692-99818-2

Introduction

I've always felt like an alien stranded in a world where I don't belong. Trying to make sense of humans is work I have spent my entire life on purely as a survival skill.

I always found strength through music, and song lyrics guided me through the murky waters of human emotion. It wasn't long before I began putting words together to make sense of things in my own way.

These pages are filled with (admittedly bastardized and Americanized) haiku: seventeen syllable observations, micro fictions and memoirs, losses and loves. They explore this world through eyes that often struggle with what they see.

These haiku are also a firsthand look at substance abuse and mental illness, a journey of recovery which highlights both the healing and the harm. It's a boy growing up, if he ever was a real boy to begin with: tending wounds and facing fears, and finally beginning to learn what it means to be part of this world instead of an outside observer.

Serving as bookends to this collection of haiku are two free verse poems, each about a "death" in my family. Both of these deaths were conscious decisions that I made. I used every tool I had available to me to make these choices, choices which have weighed heavily on my conscience. This is a kind of weight which will never be alleviated, though the burden may be eased by time, by growth, by healing, by faith, and by love. Logically, I did what I did because I had to.

There's nothing logical about faith, about love, about family, or about death.

These are forever.

"All perceptions are as mirrors,
it's your own reflections that you see."

-Aaron Weiss

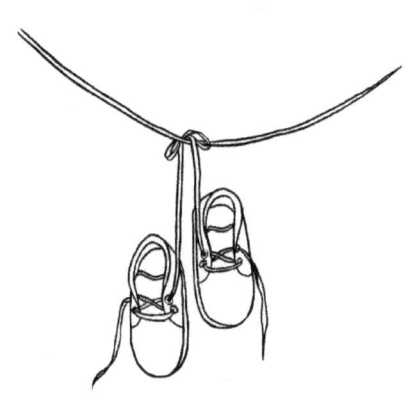

Never Worn

The snow's a blanket, cold, to counteract
the warmth inside these happy homes,
and I leave my tracks to be covered
beneath the flaky wilderness of family.
I didn't want to come home
for Christmas this year.

It's the wrong holiday
for times like these—
string lights and evergreens,
singing in suburban streets.

Through a picture window a picture perfect
father holding his sweatered son
on one knee as a claymation special graces
a widescreen TV, the mother sitting in an
armchair idly, wide-eyed and proud and happy.
The light in her eyes reminds me of the way
that you used to look at me
before that surgery.

Such a shame to need to spare the
child of the world we could provide—
street lights and sirens,
sleepless nights and unemployment lines.

I trudge grudgingly through the yard where
my childhood lies buried and up the back steps
through an unlocked door
where my mother greets me.
She asks how everything's been and I say "the
same," neglecting entirely to mention
how in October
you carried her grandchild as I cradled your
stomach and cried beside you as you slept
or how in November,
I tied a pair of baby shoes together at the lace
and tossed them over a powerline
outside the bedroom
where the little one was made:
a memorial more fitting than a grave
for someone who never had a body to box;
who was never even given a name.

Foundations

this world's built upon
Lego bricks and promises
half these things will break

Year of the Rabbit

it seems we've misplaced
the ground we're meant to sleep on
and the stars above

Elsewhere

oh! to drift from here
and into an abstraction
of where we belong

Democracy

we are all slaves here
money is the reward now
where did passion go?

No Doubt

if what you have to
say is not as beautiful
as silence, don't speak.

Brittany

I've brewed a full pot
and let half sit and go stale
ever since you left

Paddle

these are all plague rats
toss the children overboard
they will learn to swim

Walter

he cooks crystal meth
because he is good at it
because he likes it

Toasty

the best part of life
is changing out of wet socks
and into dry ones

Black Lab

passion leaves no trace
our despair is infinite
we are all hollow

Still

adrift, free of hope
tattered sails break to the cold
we'll never see home

Shelly

reach exceeding grasp
a siren on the shoreline
croons you toward the reef

Marilyn Manson

she dreamt of spacemen
burnt up in the atmosphere
she choked on ashes

Television

between the two ferns
sit a pair of dull talkers
we watch anyway

Drench

the clouds are looming
our hiding spots will dissolve
when the storm comes in

Puscifer

during spring cleaning
the vacuum took dad's ashes
please don't tell grandma

Alcoholism: Level 2

that ravenous gaze
your moist lips, my loosened tongue
we should stop drinking

Instagram

life imitates art
we're copies of photographs
it's all just pretend

Eminem

I'm sorry, doctor
the prescription has run out
and I'm still crazy.

Meme

thank you, internet
baby insanity wolf
has brightened my day

Vinnie

"damn these cement shoes,"
you cry out to the fish, as
water fills your lungs

Alcoholism: Level 5

drink until sunrise
contemplate the end of things
sleep 'til it's dark out

Fragile Creatures

we're just animals
we've clipped our claws; our teeth rot
still, we act surprised

Ishmael

huddled in corners
the last living things look on
at the mess we've left

Up

when the stars collide
we'll look back and wonder why
we wasted our time

Lapdance

the cheapest stripper
listens to all my problems
her eyes are pinholes

Vacant

alone on Christmas
in an empty laundromat
without a quarter

Weezer

a needle, some thread
to stitch the seams you've undone
with unsteady hands

Belonging

give back what you took
and nothing else will remain
all you have: stolen

Poochie

stalled in the headlights
frantic by the yellow lines
swept off of your paws

Porcupine Tree

another nice dream
life pales in comparison
so just stay asleep

Dialogue

you talk yourself down
it's conflict resolution
where nobody wins

Hours

sitting in Starbucks
my white mocha has gone cold
but I'm not finished

Writer

late night café blues
sugared lattes, blank pages
uninvited dawn

Icarus

seventh story leap
I wish that you had been there
to watch me sprout wings

The Lonely Island

you only live once
so be as careful as fuck
don't drink or use drugs

Saucony

even the best kicks
are useless in a gunfight
can't outrun bullets

Neutral Milk Hotel

and when the wolf howled
"the world screams and falls apart"
I simply believed

Listless

this is not enough
so dull, so vicarious
we should be heroes

Drive

lost on the highway
clouds obstruct the rising sun
and they're raining blood

The Saga of the Pirate Tabby Part I

last night I dreamt that
in your closet was a sea
your cat: my first mate

The Saga of the Pirate Tabby Part II

we sailed through your clothes
salt stung your best dressing gown
sorry about that

The Saga of the Pirate Tabby Part III

without a compass
out of sight of the north star
we crashed on the shore

The Saga of the Pirate Tabby Part IV

savage lands waited
they took us in, arms open
we were born again

The Saga of the Pirate Tabby Part V

but in the morning
no longer a captain, I
gazed out from the docks

Lola

guys, let's watch Space Jam
like it's nineteen ninety-eight
where's the VCR?

Drybones

you know you've killed me
you don't know that I'll haunt you
that I'll hunt you down

Another New Year: Dusk

the clock's winding down
"this will be the best year yet,"
we lie to ourselves

Another New Year: Dawn

thank god that's over.
I wish you a broken heart
and happy new year.

Honeyhive

kingdoms have been razed
strong men brought to their knees for
what's between your thighs

NYU Essay

hey, you. James Franco.
don't you think it's time you stopped?
seriously, dude.

Killing Joke

"you know, it's funny—"
(and then he pulled the trigger
but nobody laughed)

China

hands around your throat
hold you under the water
so you cannot scream

Skrillex

a banner-ad rave
I don't want light-up hoodies
and yet you persist

Jacob

the sighs; the silence
you used to be prettier
you used to care more

Thrice

someone told me once
"rhetoric can raise the dead"
it's just empty words

Oddity Market

**it's half carnival
half thrift store stockroom remorse
entirely absurd**

Peopling

it's fun to pretend
so become something you're not
'til you die alone

Stillborn

I meant to comment:
the fetus in the stork's mouth
that was a nice touch

Ouroboros

remember yourself
revive the monster you were
let it devour you

The Mountain Goats

play with gasoline
jump toward a moving train
keep yourself alive

Union Joke

What did Jesus say
to the teamsters? "Don't do a
thing 'til I get back."

Holy Ghost

atop a hillside
a specter sleeps in his home
his nightmares come true

Zaferia

you are good enough
you are attractive enough
and people like you

Gnarls Barkley

it has been on loop
the needle has worn the grooves
it's shattered my skull

Cradle to Casket

we're all scientists
replicating the same test
indefinitely

Analog

your cable's severed
your signal's interrupted
embrace the distance

The Cure

remain in my hands
don't sift through fingers like sand
this is a romance

For Aiur

I have come to serve
I'll do what you ask of me
until their hive falls

Circle

I will meet you there
at the edge of the ending
by where we began

Muse

it's like way back when
your shine stole my silences
and we were perfect

Aila

the end of the bar
houses possibilities
least of which is sleep

Rihanna

I'll come on over
start a fire in your kitchen
we'll hold hands and burn

Sink

burning aeroplane
freezing seafoam far below
inflation failure

Memphis Minnie

when the levee breaks
we will have no place to stay
also, we might drown

The Moment

future uncertain
past incurably passive
right now, there's something

Paz Lenchantin

nobody told me
Paz was playing with Pixies
you motherfuckers

Baristdemon

we are surrounded
there's no getting out of this
hope Hell serves Starbucks

Nine Inch Nails

we're spiraling wild
fate flows down the path chosen
we're still in control

Goths

those are nice black clothes.
do you feel like Darth Vader?
you're not even close.

1999 AD

the day of Lavos
came and went without a hitch
you've done well, Crono

Laura Beard

you, through the windshield
this leather's called a seatbelt
guess you never knew

Hemlock

you are all I need
you're the end of a tough time
you're something fatal

Nirvana

a rifle, a pin
a greenhouse, a thought, a loss
a big decision

Pendulum

it goes on like this
as the tide comes in; recedes
time is running out

Breathe

it's about small steps
and even the tiny ones
stop trying to leap

Climax

the machine cuts off
breathing becomes difficult
cherish these moments

Snark

the silent creature
moving throughout the shadows
feeds on your terror

Stalk

that shade moves through walls
wraps itself between your sheets
you're never lonely

Always

and if it is true
some moments last forever
let's stay in this one

Love

his sister told him
dryhumping wasn't incest
he was a weird kid

Cunning

I want to make out
with your vagina beneath
the glow of starlight

The Mars Volta

go grinding your jaw
loosen all your crooked teeth
rot from the inside

Freedom

I'm here to save you.
I am your superhero.
stay quiet and drive.

The Front Bottoms

I can't escape you
you're just like the NSA
or my student loans

Earth Day

the polluted air
waste in water; lake on fire
dead birds everywhere

Plaid Skirt

the devil touched her
and she must have enjoyed it
she asked him to stay

Departure

slip out the window
don't let anybody know
where your secrets go

Morrigu

she looks at me, asks
"what's really worth living for?"
I just turn away

Riley

your choking fetish,
eagerness and brittle bones
my long night digging

Extraction

slipping out the back
did you think no one noticed?
I saw what you did

Lifestyle

Facebook recommends
liking amateur porn stars
and top shelf liquor

Semen Stains

some girls will swallow
most of them will spit it out
but all will wonder

why this black, viscous
liquid is secreting from
their gums, and why its

flavor reminds them
of a forgotten childhood's
clouded memory

Disgorge

she's filled with secrets
sometimes her arms bend backward
and they all spill out

Lauren O'Connell

all I want is you
rocking back inside my heart
through radio waves

Sundancer

imagine dragons
at the edges of the map
they're under your bed

Slate

half drowned, post-shipwreck
sent out an S.O.S. call
you texted back nudes

Prerogative

white people standing
high above the rest of man
wasting their blessings

Bloodflowers & Jerry's

Valentine's Day rules:
Listen to The Cure alone.
Stuff ice cream in face.

Agnostic

eventually
we will shed these bonds of flesh
ascend or vanish

Elizabeth

talking to myself
over a cup of coffee
wishing you could hear

Right Away, Great Captain!

I just dreamt I was
sailing ships with Andy Hull
it was really weird.

Veracity

to master chaos:
let your life astonish you
embrace the nonsense

Disconsent

sometimes, when alone
I think of you, masturbate
and feel like a thief

Eden

she wants a new world
where the people are hopeful
and pretty things grow

Mittens

flannel pajamas
marshmallowed mugs of cocoa
eternal darkness

Hook

she stabs at my leg
says "all grown-ups are pirates"
can't really blame her

BPM

accelerating
your heart beats out of your chest
that was too much blow

Scavenger

rummage through the days
for anything worth saving
the long night is near

Quilt

people's hands have worked
in unison to stitch up
the pieces of you

At Last

treasure the time spent
waiting your turn in line when
the hangman draws near

Wild

eternal tigers
a walrus in a strange hat
interstellar wolves

Mary

oh, mewithoutYou
why not play the one about
hanging Elephant?

Navi

little light of mine
I've lost the tune of the spark
that you sang to me

Brick

blood on the skyline
the homeless, hopeless, and damned
ghosts of Central Square

Tree

brittle leaves tumble
off all of your twisted limbs
bark lets out a sigh

EarthBound

the saddest object
is a broken Nintendo
so many worlds, gone

DKC

swinging on the vines
throwing barrels at kremlings
eating bananas

Low

the bottle's empty
the medicine has run out
so, this is "sober"

Calendars

the spinning clockwork
days go by, and months then turn
bitterly to years

Mange

this is a warning
do not feed chalk to stray cats
the chalk angers them

Sandman

lay your head down now
be overcome by silence
dream of beginnings

Cain

you and me. a knife
lying between us, daring
both to make a move.

East Coast

Boston, in Autumn.
New York City in the Spring.
Winter... fuck Winter.

Timothy

I want you bound, gagged,
nailed to a cross on Main Street
and left there to rot

Revision

trapped in the Tardis
swapping out all the answers
spinning into place

Together

if you read the signs
and I ask the right questions
we might just make it

Never Leapt

standing on the ledge
considering the flight path
to concrete below

Experienced

I know this is hard
but you should listen to me
because I've been there

You Stole

a broken promise...
maybe it was just a lie.
either way, fuck you.

Afterpiece

this is curtain call
the final act of the play
hear, now, my swansong

Blemish

the package is bent
its contents compromised
yet still functional

Jaws Theme

always sad to see
what happens to the proud when
they take on the crown

Cold

leave Boston before
you act like you're a stranger
when you're with your friends

Tigress

stripes dulled and faded,
the tiger paces her cage,
tail between her legs

Casino Night

blinded by neon
that drowns out the sun itself
we toss dollars down

Nagaina

slither through the brush
venomous fangs, poison tipped
poised to strike Mongoose

Celestial

Sun blisters my skin
Moon calms my weary conscience
Stars brighten my path

Shrink

the walls edge closer
to the center of the room
the world gets smaller

Sadie

the time of your life
at the bottom of a pool
of your lover's blood

Anubis

your heart in my hands
your flesh in my frying pan
like thick-cut bacon

Nuts and Bolts

rust over our threads
things never fit right these days
time tarnished our shine

Glitch

it's dark because night
and it's cold because winter
but why scorpions?

Parka

my jacket's zipper
has broken, as if to say
"winter needs to end"

Shift

change consumes landscapes
and the animals move on.
nothing's permanent.

Spasm

it may take a while
but in the end, it's worth it:
eating that pussy.

Nightlight

vibrant as morning
the moon rose over desert
beneath brilliant stars

La Dispute

as the years go on
days feel like dress rehearsals
showtime never comes

Tara

I hate to admit:
sometimes I still see your face
in strangers outside

Grandfather

looking for answers
in the pages of this book
they lie beneath dirt

Vanilla

I had a dream where
you were baking cookies
in the dishwasher

Intervention

there is no one there
waiting in line after me.
this is your last chance.

Subjugation

naked, bound and gagged
I've never seen such beauty
in such helplessness

Spotlight

I lit some fireworks
aimed at your bedroom window
just to let you know

Thor

a day filled with clouds
where the thunder crashes in
like a derailed train

Fi

beneath willow trees
out in some forgotten grove
it has been waiting

21st Century Activist

rivers running red
with the blood of the natives
I bitch on Facebook

Locker

beneath the ocean
in places where the light won't reach
secrets stay hidden

Only

circumstances change.
people have to walk away.
you'll always have you.

Adamant

up in the arctic
a penguin learns how to fly
but you can't move on

Jumble

blood on the counter.
not sure if it's part of lunch,
or who called the cops.

Arital

the sun in her eyes
and the curves of her body,
the sand in her hair.

They Mean Everything

I wasn't made
to sit in rooms and talk like
words mean anything

Cymbal Crash

I feel mania.
man, bipolar disorder
sure has its upside.

Kink

there's a chance that things
will get really weird, real quick
and that's a good thing.

Ferguson

the streets were burning
by the spark of discontent
to the kindling mob

Afghani Blood

men in uniform
piling carcasses in sand
nobody's watching.

Luxury

setting suns can't shine
the way they do afternoons
on the porch with you

Inheritance

the long, cold storms that
led me to be what I am
began with your clouds

In/Out

I hope you love life
the way that I love to smoke.
savor every puff.

Jimmy

palm trees, clear waters
margaritas, parasols:
all just fantasy.

Forty-Eight

earth will crack open.
the sky will rain fire and stone.
and we... we will rise.

Survivalism

if it's you or me,
then it's going to be me.
nothing personal.

Easter

and the lord rose up
like turtles from the sewers
to fight for justice

Waltz

this celestial dance
always spinning in circles
just to come back 'round

Yet

someday I will be
a confident man, but that
day is not today

Jack

the edge of the knife
sparkles bright in the moonlight
as it finds its mark

Adhesive

this is a prison
it doesn't have any bars
still, I am held here

Stipulation

when I become king
I will forgive this trespass
and that's a promise

The Breakfast Club Soundtrack

I keep you, boxed up,
in a corner of the room
for when I need you

Autonomy

here, in this moment
past and all plans disposed of,
you and I are free.

Xanax

narcoleptic wives
cooking the roast in their sleep
like breathing machines

OK Cupid

we will watch Netflix
and drink until we forget
there's a world outside

Teeming

my heart's a warehouse
and there's no more space to spare
not for your bullshit

Puppy

I will come when called
I know how to use my tongue
won't you please pet me?

Nearly

ten minute warning
the oxygen will deplete,
so say your goodbyes

Squandered

I had something once.
I held it in my hands, and
now it's gone, gone, gone.

Artless

a depressed artist
not adding a single thing
to the world at all

Transmission

we crawled just like ants
touching antennae sometimes
just to stay informed

Boozer

I've got a six pack,
a shotgun, a vendetta,
poor impulse control…

Abed

Community, guys.
It was just one season and
a movie away.

Volatile

midnight on io
as if time means a thing here
this place always burns

Peach

I asked for sugar,
and she gave me her bare skin,
which was way too sweet.

Kevin Devine

the constant, bracing
shock of this fleeting moment
is overwhelming

Savage

streets were murder red
instead of their tombstone slate
and you were laughing

Blunt

my sort of kindness
strangles strangers from behind.
it shows no remorse.

The Dresden Dolls

I really don't know
how to tell anyone and
I'm sick of hiding

Agoraphobe

the walls are spinning
which seems like a real problem
because I'm outside

Berries Are Best

when I become king
I will outlaw these lemon
flavored fruit snacks. gross.

Destructor

the hard truth of it:
I want to destroy nice things,
and you can't stop me.

Murmur

I see your lips move,
and listen for the soft sound
carried on the breeze

Daisy

she says she's not sure
what living is really worth
but it's all she knows

Helen

your eyes were made of
ocean waves and foreign films
I drowned somewhere new

Independence Day

I will drink alone
for this exploding Christmas
until I feel free

Huginn

solutions include
boring the thoughts from your skull
with a power drill

The Smiths

will to live worn thin
I fantasize about sleep
in foreign places

8:55 AM

these are my mornings:
the view of this blue dumpster,
not enough coffee.

Third Eye Shut

my extra eyelid
folds over all of these things
I'd rather not see

Owl

setting sun can't shine
much longer, but the night, oh
the night shines brighter

Proposition

will you walk me home?
these streets can be dangerous
but then, so can I

There Is No Denny's

nightmares become real
at the Denny's on route one
but... bacon sundaes.

Prospects

I won't let you down,
so long as you don't expect
very much from me.

Guile

you poor, sheltered thing!
let me show you the horror
the world has in store

2001-20XX

empire in decline.
flex the muscle, flash the teeth.
fear everything.

Hannah

green eyes to your blues
arm's length terms of endearment
a rising heart rate

Reckoning

you said I was lost
but you never even asked
where I was going

Tumble

trip on untied shoes
blame a stranger for the fall
never learn a thing

Wind

our compass is shot
yet we sail ever onward
beneath starless skies

Trailer Trash

the things that you left
and all the places you went
and the child you were

Mementos

the strands of your hair
that I find in my clothing
after you are gone

Inflated

thin privilege is
a dress shirt off of the rack
fitting properly

Pretty Girls Make Graves

she's the kind of girl
who burns in holy water
and bathes in cold fire

Silencer

the best kept secrets:
between fingertips and the
notches in your spine.

Ringer Park

in this place right here
except it was 4 AM
and we were lovers

Cleaver

when the line between
the meat and butcher is blurred
we'll be skinned alive

Film

the future rewinds.
the frame sticks in the present.
the past is over.

The Postal Service

she looked ahead and
said "everything looks perfect,
just don't look too close."

The Witness

when your engines burst
and your support beams cave in
I'll watch you collapse

The Technician

when your engines burst
and your support beams cave in
I will repair you

Hallmark

we're all alone when
love comes packaged on store shelves:
those greeting card wounds.

Davy Jones

home is where the heart
is stored in a golden box
sealed by dark magic

New York Sunrise

after last call comes
the sun will rise over Queens
and the world will end

Robin WIlliams

my spark of madness
bursts like a supernova
consuming the dark

Spun

we drown like rodents
in the flood we have made of
our time and our blood

Kalsi

you're the lens through which
I can see myself the way
I probably should

30 Seconds to Mars

so, there are bridges
over rivers and bright stars
and other worlds, too.

Loveless

goodbye, my lovers.
you drink from the shining cup
I can only spill.

Lillian

>the blood spilling out
of the stork's mouth: the stillborn,
my last loss of faith.

Sarah Reiser

>the shattering glass,
twisting metal, snapped plastic,
and all of that blood.

Stifle

the way it ended.
I took it like a grown man:
aching and crying.

Patient

sobbing in pillows
for no good reason now
awaiting the end

Muninn

so, just between us
I can't sleep some nights because
I still remember.

Take the Rainbow

the gun in her mouth,
the surprise in her eyes when
it blasted Skittles

Cozy

I never miss you;
I just cherish the peace in
our long silences.

Tigers Jaw

yeah. so I was wrong.
maybe I'm a slow learner.
or a hard liver.

John Darnielle

I hope the people
who have ever done you harm
have trouble sleeping.

Syncope

waking up somewhere
you don't know, next to someone
you are afraid of

Ozymandias

I watch worlds crumble
as time lays waste to options,
to hearts, and to lungs.

Ritual

does anyone know
how to remove goat's blood from
vintage wedding gowns?

Depletion

and you'll wake up, old,
your accomplishments buried
beneath excuses.

The Grudge

no thief stole your youth,
no woman removed your heart.
you've built your own hell.

Optometry

I've been resetting
the way I see things, searching
for something clearer

Warmth

most days it's not true.
on the days when it is, though...
oh, those are the days.

Bose

renewing my ears
to hear the music again
like it's the first time

Lull

the empty spaces
in all these conversations
darken our bright days

Leviathan

I see things swimming
behind those blue eyes. the same
things lurk beneath mine.

Pummel

there are secrets stored
within the walls of this house.
go get the hammer.

Faultline

collapsing structures
screeching breaks, screaming children
the cracks in the earth

Jackal

let me taste your joy,
your pain, your shame, your ego.
let me swallow it.

Snowhead

ice aches brittle bones
there's a bitter wind blowing
we are all so cold

Burglar

take me. like a thief,
hide me deep in your pockets:
safe, secret; all yours.

Hijacker

she'd step on flowers
or shave off a lion's mane
to feel prettier

Veteran

I have been pig-piled
by screaming, biting toddlers.
I can handle this.

Daryl Palumbo

there's love, and there's that
real hard shit. but, in the end,
it's all just fucking.

Feed

those nonsense quizzes
inane political rants
stupid lists of things

Alexandra

but... bees don't have knees.
are you saying I'm nothing?!
I exist, dammit!

Dichotomy

he knocks back his drink,
says "now, I'm a feminist,
but fuck bitches, man."

LSD

then your head explodes
to watercolor worlds and
overwhelming shapes

Lucille

I had a dream that
you were still here beside me.
I woke up screaming.

Filters

we, much like lampshades
spend far too much of our time
holding our light in

Leslie

each night I pray that
the narcotics in your brain
make this go away

Tenet

consider that God
may never believe in you.
just make yourself proud.

Bright One

of all the voices
rambling in my head, yours is
making the most sense.

Kaitlyn

disillusionment
strikes in the strangest moments.
I never loved you.

Mantra

the stories we tell
to convince ourselves of the
lies we need to live

Trauma

accidents happen
and then you're scarred forever
psychologically

Finite

it happens too late:
realizing the money's not
worth the price you've paid.

Empath

even when my brain
is in the off position,
I still care too much.

Keyless

all the doors are locked
wind rattles our mourning bones
the concrete is cold

Deftones

sand between your toes;
the sun beating down on you.
beware the water.

Changing Lanes

counting down the days
'til inevitable change.
I should start over.

Suffocate

the killing of gods:
mankind takes its final breath,
choking on its sword.

Sootsprites

your head will pulsate
as dark things scurry and nest
deep inside your skull

Pink Floyd

I have built this wall
day by day and brick by brick.
only you got through.

Combustion

on my bus ride home
she is engulfed by her book
and I fall in love

My Bloody Valentine

there are things I've done
that would make you cringe, yet more
that would make you smile

Cement

maybe you'll go home
but you will never, ever
get away from here

Alcoholism: Level 12

I fear my liver
has simply ceased functioning.
can't say I blame it.

Alcoholism: Boss Fight

the hole in my heart
leads to unfiltered whiskey
running through my veins

Junkyard Wolves I

hush. keep your voice down.
don't even breathe. they'll hear you.
they are so hungry.

Junkyard Wolves II

the flesh in their teeth.
the ecstatic yelps and howls.
so, this is the end.

Junkyard Wolves III

the dumpster hounds strike.
there isn't any struggle.
it's a massacre.

Junkyard Wolves IV

their glacial blue eyes
sparkling beneath the streetlights
shimmer remorseless.

Michael

water fills your lungs.
I'd say "I'm sorry," but
I'd do it again.

Oui

a fond memory:
us in a room together
before this whole mess

Clint Mansell

back where it started:
that shack behind the drugstore
where innocence slipped

Crossing

I should never have
walked over that bridge, nor slit
its slackline supports.

Daughter

I still think of you
though you never had a name
and never arrived

Carissa's Wierd

you always loved green.
fitting: a rope from a tree.
I'll miss you the most.

Polyamorous Children

it's almost over.
things got pretty weird in here.
who goes home with who?

Hoarder

at least you've still got
a box full of your mistakes
and some old receipts.

Loki

you could be the best
place that I have ever been
or an old nightmare.

Moist

feel like a teen girl
at a One Direction show:
I am soaking wet.

Second Sons

you asked what I want.
I want you to hate yourself
the way I hate mine.

Parabox

there's another place
where things that went wrong here
all went right instead.

Looper

it's no way to live
yet here we are, doing it
every single day

Against Me!

we make up our beds
for these secrets to sleep in
as we pace the room

Ash

though I watched you change
as flames consumed your body
I know you're still here

Effie Harrington

I'd meant to write you
a letter, to tell you it
couldn't be that bad.

Nude

through the raging winds
the cold tore through our old skin,
exposed what we were.

Arf Arf

wolven gravity
pulls you down with claptrap jaws
you're canine breakfast

Pale

if we edit out
all of the darker pieces
we won't know the light

Stitchery

it will take all day
to undo the damage done.
we'll sleep well tonight.

Exhale

over the machines
I could almost make it out:
your final farewell

At the Drive-In

with violent strokes
I will cover your silence
in relentless sound

Unforgivable

it's far too late now.
you don't come back from that one.
there's no coming back.

Balance and Composure

aggression subsides.
that jealous heartbeat will slow.
she'll never love you.

Northern Wild

those trembling chilled limbs
snowblind in the clutch of cold
you won't make it home.

Simple

maybe you'll waste your
whole life waiting for something
better to happen

Joni

you're too tightly strung
and the walls are folding in
and nothing feels right

Glassjaw

wish they'd figure out
how to shrink stars so I can
keep one in my room

Surya

daylight is burning
concrete desert boils beneath
unforgiving sun

Vale

the hallway's growing.
expanding; infinite. it
calls out. then it screams.

Goodbye

I'm sorry to say
this just isn't working out.
this has got to stop.

Law

there are so many
things you just can't change unless
you're an alchemist

Peter

an apparition
stalks you in daylight. oh wait,
that's just your shadow.

Morrissey

there's being alone,
and then there's that sickness that
makes you want to be.

Shia LaBeouf

look into Shia's soul.
see the misery; the joy:
Shia is all things.

You

I tried to love you.
I tried to be supportive.
I tried and I failed.

Me

You tried to love me.
You tried to be supportive.
You tried and you failed.

I Can't See the Stage

stop taking pictures
with your phone. just stop taking
pictures with your phone.

Pack

I can't forgive you.
you can't forgive me, either.
so get the hell out.

Evanescence

the days grind down on
the soul; the heart disconnects
but beats on, emptied.

The Slip

by accident, we
slit the throats of our captors
and ran toward the light

Authentic

for the first time, I'm
sure this is no false alarm.
this is happening.

Sever

it's a good season
for moving objects; people.
for burning bridges.

Therapy

escort agencies;
brothels disguised as hotels:
someone to listen.

Ideals

we muttered phrases
about better worlds; kingdoms
that would never come

Widower

that old coyote caught
his roadrunner; blew him up;
lost all sense of self.

Bookends

rummage through attics.
try to find that thing you lost:
who you used to be.

Sacrifice

get up off your knees
transform into your own god
worship. pay tribute.

mewithoutYou

I can see God where
you won't dare to look; in words
you won't even speak.

Nintendo

touch fuzzy, dizzy
blurs the image, twists it up
a swing and a miss

broke block dinosaur
eggs rolling down hills, become
one: the two undone

echoes of extra
lives flushed down the pit; sewer
pipe warp zone silence

a hasty retreat
the flip of a lid, armored
bullet bill glides out

we run for our lives
we head for the shrines: toadstool
hotel vacancy

lakitus throw spines;
the ape in the trees: barrel
tosser in a tie

just run to the right
advance to the next level
keep running. keep right.

The Departed

Mark Wahlberg is the
greatest actor ever to
grace the stage or screen

My Morning Jacket

my morning jacket
is much like my evening frock:
it's the same jacket.

Coloring Book

just show me something.
show me anything at all;
anything worthwhile.

Electric Mayhem

sorry to tell you:
it's time to meet the Muppets.
you will not survive.

Famine

deformed dogs howl in
the heart of nuclear winter
aching for a meal

Paved

there is nothing where
so many things used to be.
there's nothing at all.

Apart

am I the wave that
breaks against the stone, or the
stone that salt erodes?

Solace

discarded prayer
a fond, distant memory
unburdened silence

Miley Cyrus

I will never love
anyone other than you
and that's terrible.

Ensign

if you stare at the
ISIS flag long enough, you
can see a sailboat

Tool

the believer asks
"why must my shoulders carry
the burden of proof?"

The End of Time

there's a lamp post out
in the middle of nothing
and it's the way home

Contact

I've never believed,
but I've wanted to. I've tried.
I just can't see it.

City Sleeps

the endless pavement
blankets far more than just trees
it covers our dreams

Frame

the picture might not
fit the way you want it to.
nothing ever does.

Parasites

you need to starve the
things inside of you that are
tearing you apart

The Boy Who Could Fly

soaring aimlessly
through the night sky with no one
to share the stars with

Sister

I only know how
to love somebody when they're
on the floor crying

Landslide

the record's spinning
out a place you used to know
and can never return

Reconstruction

still asking yourself
"are you now more together
for coming apart?"

Saul Williams

they unlocked the cage
but without the means to survive
you're still in prison.

Shift

the clock will flicker
between never and always
you: caught in its midst

Advanced Optics

the world seems ugly,
but I'm still afraid to die.
I should look harder.

Cloud

there's a better half
you can no longer see. that
does not mean it's gone.

Irishman at Grendel's Den

"you should dream bigger.
don't you know that dreams are free
when nothing else is?"

Tick-Tock

the clock keeps ticking
even when you can't hear it.
never forget that.

Flea

you can't keep hiding.
you're two kids in a trench coat.
someone will notice.

Slash

sift through the wreckage.
nothing of value remains.
don't linger. move on.

Ozzie

those who know don't talk.
the rest keep their mouths moving.
those who talk don't know.

Reapers

we harvest the souls
of our lovers, children; friends
to nourish our own

Cunt

damn it. god damn it.
jesus fucking christ. damn it.
damn it. damn it. shit.

Squall

you sigh. the clouds come.
your sorrow rains deafening.
you drown out the world.

Eva-Marie

I say that I don't
love you anymore but I
am still a liar

Radiohead

I've wasted my life
all strung out at the gallows
watching witches burn

Twigs

she had some horses
so she tied one to his arms;
one to his legs. "run."

Evolve

hope in a stork's mouth
the withered will be replaced
we will keep going

Crime In Stereo

I watch you struggle,
you resent me when I wince.
this love drags us down.

Alcoholism: Final Credits

I used to drink like
answers were at the bottom
of the next bottle.

Cherry Coke

you're the same old dog
you were back then. new tricks don't
change the howling heart.

Tony

our aching muscles;
the years that brought us this pain;
the path we walk, still.

Lunch

I am the largest
of the monsters in this room.
what does that make you?

Shown

she sees the scars, says
"something's better than nothing"
we know. we both know.

Shone

she sees the stars, says
"something's better than nothing"
we know. we just do.

Rouse

there are trees growing
in forests you've never seen
the world's still breathing

Yellow

thriving in our throats
on pages of books; the drapes:
these nicotine stains.

Zippo

some flints and fluid
the signs we send with our sparks
and steel precision

Keeper

I sliced you open
stuffed you with my secrets, sewed
up your plush belly

AJJ

when I'm a dead boy,
turn my ashes into trees.
don't sell my records.

Rose

seven frail petals
a single thorn on the stem
all the love there is

Cannibal

I swallowed my eyes
to see my stomach's contents.
there, I found your heart.

Kush

I watched the smoke float
from the lungs of a lover
to infinite space

A Perfect Circle

we have pulled ourselves
up and out of worse than this.
hold fast. choose to live.

Skeletal

you're the mystery guest
in a haunted hotel room
or some costume ball

Tuesday

making art on the
really bad days is too hard.
fuck this nonsense, right?

Alkaline Trio

there may be whiskey
on my breath but that doesn't
mean I don't love you

Veil

my oblivion
consists of you, shining stars,
and red Mountain Dew.

Industry

filling our stomachs
one way or another
we empty our hearts

Do Not Disturb

there are some spiders
their webs crawl up the doorway
no one passes through

Phoenix

disaster rises
from expectations' ashes
scorching what remains

Comet

I watched stars die:
laser lights on velvet skies
dancing through the night

Reveal

stretched to the sidelines
the center begins to crack
to a crooked smile

Artemis

you're the brightest star
of all the light reflections
glinting overhead

Autumn

our hooded sweatshirts
a chill in the evening air
rust on fallen leaves

Dentistry

a pair of pliers
to pull all these rotten teeth.
Tylenol for pain.

Effervescent

a shine that steals us
away from our own darkness
and fills up our hearts

Indentations

the places you hid
when all the streets flooded
and the house fires burned

Oh My God

this is happening.
you elected Donald Trump.
oh god. fuck. oh god.

Trumped

it's not a joke, guys
not anymore. it won't be
funny ever, now.

Boston

when my chalk outline
at last circles this city
how will you feel it?

Evermore

this goes beyond us
through childhood bedroom windows
ceaselessly toward caskets

Brother

I watched you watch me
as we shook outside ourselves
between our darkness

Roots

aqua seafoam shame
hanging from the curtain rods
of cellar windows

The Movielife

pack up the pieces.
wait at the side of the road
for the bus to come.

Anticipation

I thought that you were
ignoring the text message
I forgot to send

Marvin Gaye

someone told me once
"only love can conquer hate"
well... love and pipe bombs.

Narrative

soak in illusion
chew on the world you've been fed
try not to swallow

My Chemical Romance

I've been an addict,
an alcoholic, and a
criminal. so what?

Brandon Laterneau

there's a light rainfall
there's a gentle wind blowing
heroin is bad

Saige

your whisper echoed
'round my sweet insanity
like a warm blanket

David Bowie

she stepped from the ledge
eyes were blue but no one home
she met the concrete

Growth

I just cannot wait
to be dead and in the ground
feeding the topsoil

Psychosis

they're shadow people.
they live in the dark corners.
you should be afraid.

Archers of Loaf

lungs are submerged deep
the water is red, red, red
the sun vanishes

Fuzz

I can hear static
drowning out all of the things
that aren't worth hearing

Rock 'n' Roll Suicide

you're a dying star.
the bile building in your throat
is suffocating.

Trickledown

you placed the burden
on the shoulders of the weak;
blamed them for collapse

Kharon

coins over my eyes
I can pay for the ferry
take me somewhere nice

Cortisol

synapse disconnect.
stripped bare, the joint will not thread.
there's no going back.

Brand New

if you are without
well I am just full of it
so take some of mine

April 15

sinking in pavement
this concrete castle's gates close
nobody gets out

Aunt

I've been rushing 'round
and sifting through this whole mess
just to hold a ghost

Grune

Thundercats are on
the move. Thundercats are loose.
That one has rabies.

Molly

finally. your flesh
in my hands. your lips reach mine.
oh, how I waited.

I Am A Nightmare

when I fell asleep
holding your hand I was sure
I'd wake up happy

Probius

your zerglings are weak.
this is a motherfucking
probe rush, you bitches.

Poor

we crept like insects
in the dark to kitchen floors
searching out your scraps

Amygdala

there's something I lost
I never knew what it was
but I want it back

Smashing Pumpkins

considerately,
we will fade away, drift off
to oblivion

(45)

I read the paper
and then I cry my eyes out
every single day.

Ninety-Seven Years

All that I want is
Mulan Szechuan dipping sauce
for my McNuggets.

Dread

if there's always hope
then where the fuck does it hide
in the midst of this?

Lizzy

your hair reminds me
of feet dipping in oceans;
salt smells of summer

Fool

seconds pass; minutes.
hours become days, months, and years.
it all ends in dust.

Renewal

so I burned your name
written on an index card,
left ash to the wind.

Reflection

a small guiding light
provided by the displaced
bleeds through the shadow

Odin

you'll conjure your crows
to peck out both my eyes and
I'll see everything

Risen

when you send your brains
flying against your ceiling
where will your soul go?

Kraken

a storm coming in
a cold unforgiving sea
monsters wade beneath

Manchester Orchestra

if you knew I was
dying, would it change you? would
it change anything?

Global Mourning

you don't understand.
this is the last chance we have.
you're fucking it up.

The Model Cafe

it tastes like ashtrays
when we kiss, liquor, and some
insincerity

Crusader

take down enemies
don't let them see you crying
for their families

Fix

pencil eraser.
white out. a roll of duct tape.
undo the damage.

Meghan

the way you purse your
lips when you're contemplating
makes this sore heart skip

Cuddle

when the smell of their
sweat seems sweeter than perfume
try to hold them close

Bright Eyes

why spend so much time
wondering where your soul goes
when it's here right now?

June

This has been the best
Father's Day I've ever had.
Did not see my dad.

Iron and Wine

we will plant these seeds
in hopes that something will grow,
that it will survive.

Age

the hourglass empties
and stars die, the cold consumes
our delicate forms

Touch

find sanctuary
in the pages of books; in
the arms of strangers

Convectuoso

though you are the meat,
I will not be your butcher.
I will do no harm.

Pool

I saw my image
looking back from a red sky
as I stared straight down

The Used

left in a drawer
like old clothes that once fit but
never will again

Kristin

I have a folder
filled with nudes that look enough
like you to pretend

My Terrible Friend

when I am sent down
the plank, sing me a rainbow
and steal me a dream

Backstage

burnt out in our chairs
as guitars feed back, the crowd
roars in ecstasy

Afterhours

there will be dancing
in dimly lit city streets
long after bedtime

I Am The Avalanche

can this really be
happening? is that the sun
finally shining?

Donald Holborn

I never thanked you.
I never said "goodbye" or
"I love you." I do.

Repair

rearranging the
pieces of my life, hoping
to make them all fit

Mother

you can't undo the
damage so deep that the wound
never stopped bleeding

Family

I screamed at windows.
you believed I was crazy
and you still loved me.

Faith

we're all part of this
universe soaring on the
back of a turtle

Schism

the weekend my father died
I sat in the cemetery
waiting for him to rise,
writhing in the dirt with my demons
for three long nights.
when he didn't come back,
I counted the parts of him that I had left
and came up with the lonesome sum
of the misogynistic liquor on my breath.
when it started to rain and got cold,
I finally decided to wander home
but there was no such place anymore,
so I just stumbled down the road
to a house I had no use for.
it was my father's house once,
as was the cross on its door.
I took it down and told Christ
he didn't have to live there anymore.

Father

I could recognize
deception when I saw it, and
it flared in your eyes

Scarecrow

stuffed to the brim with
scraps of discarded terror
where is my courage?

Modest Mouse

if a time comes when
floating on is not enough
just let it capsize

Catariña

basement shows you played
rekindled a flame once bright
but long since smoldered

Neshi

when I see myself
stand beside you it is clear
who I could have been

Pink Cloud

will you listen for
the melody? one of eight
which has forged your fate?

Pet

memorize the scars
your tiger left stripping the
names from your demons

Dragon

a kindred spirit
bolsters a heart silenced by
fear of its own beat

Magic

from Allah to Zeus:
earth, fire, air, water, spirit.
you have to believe.

J.R.W.

I was the gift you
wouldn't return, now I'm a
king you'll never serve

Grey

I became myself
when within I balanced the
dark side and the light

Acknowledgements

Thank you to the visual artists who contributed to this book and its design. Cover artwork by Simon Meredith. Interior artwork by Kristen Miologos and Racknar Teyssier.

Thank you to my family, whether their names are Whipple, Mangan, Kumpf, Johnson, Sanders, Sundancer or something else I've failed to mention. Thank you to the friends who have been just as supportive as family. Thank you to Jeremy Tyarks, Elizabeth Szyman, Meghan Vortherms, and Anita Kalsi; thank you to Michael Dewar for being my most reliable reader and editor since before this book was even an idea.

Thank you to my teachers and sources of inspiration. It would take a forest to make a complete list, so I'll keep this one brief. Thank you to Catherine Parnell, Askold Melnyczuk, Joseph Torra, Joyce Peseroff, Jill McDonough, Aaron Weiss, Jesse Lacey, Daryl Palumbo, Andy Hull, James Keenan and Kevin Devine.

Thank you to the old gods and the new.

Thank you for reading.

contact:

jessereywhipple@gmail.com
jessereywhipple.tumblr.com

www.ingramcontent.com/pod-product-compliance
Lightning Source LLC
Chambersburg PA
CBHW022109090426
42743CB00008B/774